**Quick Start Guides**

C000281334

The Essenti...
SUGAR FREE
DIET
Meals For One

A Quick Start Guide
To Cooking
Sugar-Free Meals
For One

Simple And Delicious Calorie Counted Recipes For One Person.
Lose Weight And Improve Your Health.

First published in 2016 by Erin Rose Publishing

Text and illustration copyright © 2016 Erin Rose Publishing

Design: Julie Anson

ISBN: 978-1-911492-04-7

A CIP record for this book is available from the British Library.

DISCLAIMER: This book is for informational purposes only and not intended as a substitute for the medical advice, diagnosis or treatment of a physician or qualified healthcare provider. The reader should consult a physician before undertaking a new health care regime and in all matters relating to his/her health, and particularly with respect to any symptoms that may require diagnosis or medical attention.

While every care has been taken in compiling the recipes for this book we cannot accept responsibility for any problems which arise as a result of preparing one of the recipes. The author and publisher disclaim responsibility for any adverse effects that may arise from the use or application of the recipes in this book. Some of the recipes in this book include nuts and eggs. If you have an egg or nut allergy it's important to avoid these.

CONTENTS

Recipes

The Essential Sugar Free Diet Meals for One

SWEETS, DESSERTS & SNACKS

INTRODUCTION

Sticking to a healthy, sugar-free diet has just gotten easier! If you are cooking for one person and whether you are looking to expand your recipes for sugar-free cooking or maintain your sugar-free diet, then The Essential Sugar-Free Diet Meals For One is for you!

This book is ideal for anyone starting to detox from sugar and provides everyone, even experienced sugar-free chefs, with an abundance of delicious, nutritious, mouth-watering recipes especially tailored for one person. Losing weight and improving your health by cutting out sugar from your diet can be enjoyable when you have easy to prepare, fast and healthy foods to look forward too.

In this book, we provide you with a wide range of recipes, from soups and roasts to desserts and baking so there really is something for everyone. Plus many of the recipes are low in carbohydrates to really boost your weight loss and help balance your blood sugar.

A vast number of people have already felt the benefit of kicking the sugar habit and maintaining a sugar-free diet. It's not just a fad – the results speak for themselves. If you are ready to switch to a healthier diet, you can easily do so with a few pointers on how to avoid the hidden sugar trap. There is no better time to start your sugar-detox and kick start your healthy lifestyle than now!

Foods To Avoid

Don't Eat These:

Avoid or reduce your intake of any food containing sugars.

- Avoid all concentrated fruit juices, cordials, sports drinks and fizzy drinks, including diet drinks with artificial sweeteners.

- Avoid dried fruit, including apricots, dates, raisins, sultanas, mango, pineapple and figs.

- Pure or concentrated fruit juices.

- Cakes, cookies, biscuits, chocolate bars, muesli, granola, muffins, cereal bars and sweets.

- Breakfast cereals (where sugar has been added).

- Honey

- Golden syrup

- Jams and spreads

- Maple syrup

- Treacle

- Molasses

- Ready-made sauces like relishes, marinates and coatings such as sweet chilli sauce, ketchup and barbecue sauce which contain sugars.

- Ciders, beers, liqueurs, cocktails, dessert wine and mixers. Gin, vodka and dry wine have a lower sugar content.

Foods You Can Eat

You can eat the following foods. Keep fruit to a maximum of two pieces a day as it does contain fruit sugar (fructose). Tropical fruits do have a higher sugar intake so these are best avoided or eaten in moderation. You can snack on high protein foods like nuts, seeds, cold meat cuts and yogurt which will help prevent hunger and sugar cravings.

- All meats, including chicken, pork, ham, lamb, turkey and beef.

- All fish and shellfish including tinned sardines, mackerel and tuna.

- Nuts and seeds, including Brazils, hazelnuts, almonds, cashews, macadamias, peanuts, pine nuts, coconut, pecans, sunflower seeds, flaxseeds, chia, sesame and pumpkin seeds.

- Tofu, beans and pulses.

- Cheese, milk, butter, fresh cream, crème fraîche and yogurt.

- Eggs

- Nut butters including peanut, almond and cashew nut butter.

- All fresh vegetables (note; beetroot, sweet potato, carrots and onions are higher in sugar so avoid too much of these.)

- Raspberries, apples, oranges, strawberries, bananas, blackberries, redcurrants, blueberries, kiwi, blackberries, rhubarb, limes and lemons.

- Rice, corn, oats, quinoa and wholemeal bread (check label for added sugar.)

- Popcorn

- Tea, coffee, herbal and fruit teas (always check for added sugar.)

- Coconut oil, olive oil, ghee.

- Herbs, spices, garlic, salt and pepper.

Safe Sweeteners

Seeing the words 'sugar-free' on the label of a food product will usually indicate that the sugar content has been replaced by an artificial sweetener which doesn't make it a healthy substitute for harmful refined sugars.

Artificial sweeteners like aspartame, saccharin and sucralose are chemical, industrially produced additives which contain no calories, taste very sweet and are added to foods, drinks and medicines.

Artificial sweeteners have caused great controversy for years and have been linked to obesity and chronic illnesses including cancer. Despite conflicting reports on the safety of these sweeteners and their inability to be digested by the body, therefore stored in fat cells, they are still being added to common everyday foods.

Some of the recipes in this book include the use of a natural plant based sweetener called stevia (Stevia Rebaudiana) to impart sweetness to recipes, providing you with the healthiest alternative to sugar.

> **Reducing your sugar intake is beneficial to most people however always check with your medical adviser or doctor before embarking on any radical dietary changes, especially if you are diabetic or are on medication which may need to be monitored or adjusted.**

Tracking Down The Hidden Sugars

When you are shopping, always read the labels for products containing hidden sugars, listed under an alias name. You'd be surprised just how many common products contain stealth sugars, even savoury foods, so familiarise yourself with the following list. Avoiding obvious sugars is essential and bear in mind that even small quantities of hidden sugar can really add up.

Agave nectar	**Fructose**
Barley malt	**Fructose corn syrup**
Beet sugar	**Fructose syrup**
Brown sugar	**Glucose**
Cane juice crystals	**Glucose syrup**
Caramel	**Golden syrup**
Carob syrup	**Invert sugar syrup**
Coconut sugar	**Malt syrup**
Corn syrup and high fructose	**Maltodextrin**
Date syrup	**Maple syrup**
Dehydrated fruit juice	**Molasses**
Dextrin	**Palm sugar**
Dextrose	**Refiner's syrup**
Ethyl maltol	**Sucrose**
Fruit juice concentrate	**Turbinado**

Sugar-Free Cooking For One Person

- Making good use of your freezer will make life so much easier. Store chicken breasts in individual freezer bags which will prevent them sticking together. Shape minced beef into meatballs before you freeze which will provide you with an individual portion to be added to sauces or vegetable dishes.

- It's not uncommon to have left over dairy produce like milk, cream and crème fraîche when you're cooking for one, but don't let it stop you expanding your range of recipes. These can all be frozen and can easily be added to recipes. Always make sure you stir them well to avoid splitting and re-heat them thoroughly. Generally speaking, dairy products with a higher fat content such as double cream (heavy cream) freezes better than single cream because of its higher fat content. Small portions of butter and grated cheese make great store cupboard essentials when frozen and mean you won't have to pop out to the shops when they're needed in a recipe. Yogurt can be frozen into individual portions and makes a delicious breakfast or desert when combined with fresh fruit.

- Make multiple quantities of your favourite soups and casseroles and freeze them into individual portions so you have a fast tasty meal which can be defrosted quickly in the microwave. Always make sure you heat them through thoroughly before eating.

- Many of the recipes require the use of tinned tomatoes or pulses which come in larger portions but the remainder can be frozen so you avoid any waste. You can also do this with fresh vegetables or fruits which you don't want to discard. Those with a high water content can somewhat mushy when defrosted but to get around this you can puree them before freezing and/or add them to soups, stews, sauces or smoothies.

- Apart from freezing leftovers you can store leftover meats, cheese or vegetables in the fridge for a day or two and add them to stir-fries and omelettes. Some of the tastiest dishes can be rustled up from a selection of leftovers, saving you both time and money.

- Chop up any leftover fresh herbs, pop them into an ice cube tray and top it up with a little water then freeze them. They make a great flavour addition to casseroles and soups whilst avoiding waste.

- If you've overbought fresh vegetables, simply freeze them. Roasted vegetables can be made straight from frozen, the trick is to make sure your oven is hot so that they cook quickly, evaporating excess moisture preventing them from lingering in any liquid they produce.

- Once food is in the freezer it tends to look very similar to make life easier by labelling your freezer bags clearly and adding the date.

- Sometimes it can be more economical to cook batches or make extras, especially when it comes to baking. If you're concerned that you'll over indulge you can always split it or swap healthy treats with a friend. If it tastes too good to give away you can always freeze it!

Breakfast

Serrano Ham & Basil Savoury Muffins

Ingredients

25g (1oz) Serrano ham, chopped
2 large eggs
1 teaspoon butter
1 teaspoon fresh basil leaves, chopped

SERVES 1

241 calories per serving

Method

Crack the eggs into a large mug and whisk them with a fork. Add in the butter, ham and basil. Place the mug in a microwave and cook on full power for 30 seconds. Stir and return it to the microwave for another 30 seconds, stir and cook for another 30-60 seconds or until the egg is set. Serve it in the mug. Experiment with other ingredients, like chicken, bacon, beef, cheese and spring onions (scallions).

Raspberry, Ginger & Cashew Nut Crunch

Ingredients

100g (3½ oz) plain Greek yogurt
50g (2oz) raspberries
25g (1oz) unsalted cashew nuts, chopped
¼ teaspoon ground ginger

SERVES 1

291
calories
per serving

Method

Mash together half of the raspberries and all of the ginger with the yogurt. Using a glass, place a layer of yogurt with half of the remaining raspberries and a sprinkling of chopped cashews, followed by another layer of the same until you reach the top of the glass.

Almond Choc Chip Breakfast Bowl

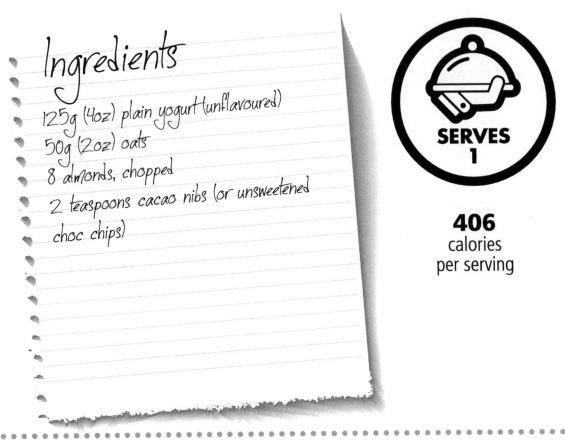

Ingredients

- 125g (4oz) plain yogurt (unflavoured)
- 50g (2oz) oats
- 8 almonds, chopped
- 2 teaspoons cacao nibs (or unsweetened choc chips)

**SERVES
1**

406
calories
per serving

Method

Place the oats in a bowl and stir in the yogurt. Sprinkle in the chopped almonds and chocolate chips. Serve and enjoy. This can also be made the night before and chilled in the fridge until morning.

Coffee & Nut Butter Protein Shake

Ingredients

250mls (8fl oz) full-fat milk
1 teaspoon instant coffee powder
1 teaspoon smooth peanut butter
1/4 teaspoon stevia sweetener (optional)
1 tablespoon vanilla whey protein powder
(sugar-free)
Several ice cubes

SERVES 1

224
calories
per serving

Method

Place all of the ingredients into blender or food processor and blitz until smooth. Serve into a glass and enjoy!

Coconut & Cucumber Smoothie

SERVES 1

118
calories
per serving

Ingredients

1 apple, cored
1/4 cucumber
Juice of 1/2 lemon
250mls (8fl oz) coconut water

Method

Place all of the ingredients into a blender and blitz until smooth. Serve straight away.

Green Detox Smoothie

Ingredients

¼ bulb of fennel, chopped
½ cucumber, chopped
1 stalk of celery
Juice of 1 lemon

**SERVES
1**

56
calories
per serving

Method

Place all of the ingredients into a food processor or smoothie maker and pour in enough water to cover the ingredients. Process until smooth.

Carrot & Blackberry Smoothie

Ingredients

100g (3½ oz) blackberries
1 carrot
1 small orange
Pinch of cinnamon

**SERVES
1**

95
calories
per serving

Method

Place all the ingredients into a blender with enough water to cover them and process until smooth.

Banana & Coconut Smoothie

Ingredients

1 banana

2 tablespoons plain (unflavoured) Greek yogurt

75mls (3fl oz) coconut milk

75mls (3fl oz) water

SERVES 1

317 calories per serving

Method

Toss all the ingredients into a blender and blitz. Pour and enjoy!

Summer Berry Smoothie

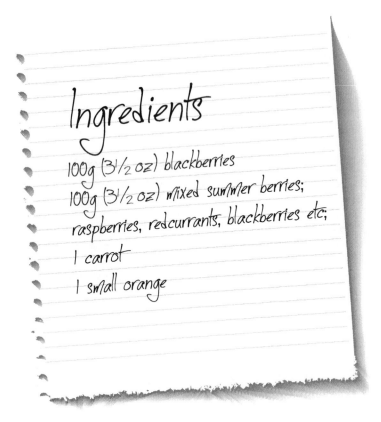

Ingredients

100g (3½ oz) blackberries
100g (3½ oz) mixed summer berries;
raspberries, redcurrants, blackberries etc;
1 carrot
1 small orange

**SERVES
1**

107
calories
per serving

Method

Place all the ingredients into a blender with enough water to cover them and process until smooth.

Ricotta & Apple Omelette

Ingredients

25g (3oz) ricotta cheese

2 eggs, beaten

1 apple, peeled, cored and finely sliced

2 teaspoons olive oil

Ground cinnamon

SERVES 1

303
calories
per serving

Method

Heat the oil in a frying pan. Add the apple to the pan and cook it until the slices become soft. Remove and set aside. Combine the beaten eggs and ricotta cheese in a bowl and mix well. Pour the egg mixture into the hot pan and while it begins to set, scatter the cooked apple over the top. Once the egg mixture has set, serve it onto a plate. Sprinkle with a little cinnamon.

Low Carb Strawberry Pancakes & Cream

SERVES 1

513
calories
per serving

Ingredients

50g (2oz) ground almonds (almond flour/almond meal)
2 eggs, whisked
60mls (2fl oz) water
1 teaspoon olive oil
5 medium strawberries, halved
1 tablespoon crème fraîche
Strawberries to garnish

Method

Combine all of the ingredients in a bowl except the oil, strawberries for the garnish and crème fraîche. Heat the oil in a frying pan and add some of the pancake batter to the size you require. Once bubbles begin to appear in the mixture turn it onto the other side. Repeat for the remaining mixture. Dollop the crème fraîche on top and scatter some strawberries on top to garnish. Serve and eat straight away.

Tomato, Feta & Basil Omelette

Ingredients

25g (1oz) feta cheese, crumbled
2 eggs
1 tomato, chopped
1 spring onion (scallion), finely chopped
1 small bunch of fresh basil, chopped
2 teaspoons olive oil
Sea salt
Freshly ground black pepper

SERVES 1

292
calories
per serving

Method

Place the feta, basil, tomato and spring onion (scallion) in a bowl and season with salt and pepper. In a separate bowl, whisk the eggs. Heat the oil in a frying pan and pour in the beaten eggs and allow them to set. Once they begin to firm up, scatter the feta/tomato mixture on one side of the omelette. Fold the other half over the top and let it warm for around a minute. Serve and eat straight away.

Cheesy Pesto Scrambled Eggs

Ingredients

2 eggs, whisked
25g (1oz) cheddar cheese, grated
(shredded)
½ teaspoon pesto
2 teaspoons olive oil
Sea salt
Freshly ground black pepper

SERVES 1

334
calories
per serving

Method

In a bowl, combine the eggs, cheese and pesto and season with salt and pepper. Heat the oil in a frying pan. Pour in the egg mixture and stir until the eggs are soft but set.

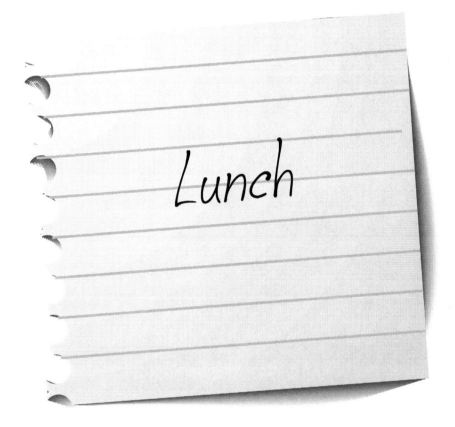

Lunch

Szechuan Turkey Salad

Ingredients

1 turkey breast, cut into strips
1/4 cucumber, deseeded and chopped
1 handful of coriander (cilantro) leaves, chopped
1/4 teaspoon ground Szechuan pepper
1 teaspoon sesame oil
2 spring onions (scallions), chopped
Juice of 1/2 lime
1 large handful mixed lettuce leaves
1 teaspoon olive oil

**SERVES
1**

281
calories
per serving

Method

Heat the olive oil in a pan, add the turkey strips and cook for 8-10 minutes or until they are completely cooked. Remove from the heat and allow it to cool. Place the cucumber and coriander (cilantro) in a bowl with the turkey. Place the sesame oil, Szechuan pepper, lime juice, spring onions (scallions) in a separate bowl then mix it with the turkey and cucumber. Serve the lettuce onto plates and spoon the turkey on top.

Smoked Mackerel
& Mushrooms

Ingredients

75g (3oz) mushrooms, sliced
1 mackerel fillet
1 tablespoon fresh parsley, chopped
1 teaspoon olive oil

**SERVES
1**

243
calories
per serving

Method

Place the fish under a hot grill (broiler) and cook for around 6 minutes turning halfway through. In the meantime heat the olive oil in a pan, add the chopped mushrooms and cook for 5 minutes until softened. Sprinkle with parsley and serve the fish and mushrooms onto plates.

Lemon & Basil Chicken Skewers

SERVES 1

357 calories per serving

Ingredients

150g (4oz) chicken breast, cut into chunks
1 small bunch of basil
1 clove of garlic, chopped
Juice of ½ lemon
1 tablespoon olive oil
Sea salt
Freshly ground black pepper

Method

Place the oil, chopped basil, garlic and lemon juice in a bowl and mix well. Add the chicken to the marinade and stir well, covering the chicken completely in the mixture. Season with salt and pepper. Slide the chicken chunks onto metal skewers. Place them under a hot grill (broiler) or barbeque and cook for 5-6 minutes on each side or until the chicken is completely cooked through. Serve on its own or with rice salad or dips.

Wild Rice Salad

Ingredients

75g (3oz) tinned mixed beans, drained
50g (2oz) tinned sweetcorn, drained
50g (2oz) brown basmati rice
25g (1oz) wild rice
2 spring onions (scallions), finely chopped
1/2 red pepper (bell pepper), finely chopped
1 small bunch fresh coriander (cilantro), finely chopped
Juice of 1/2 lime
Pinch of chilli flakes (optional)
Sea salt
Freshly ground black pepper

**SERVES
1**

394
calories
per serving

Method

Cook the rice according to the instructions. This may need to be done separately if the cooking times are different as wild rice usually takes longer to cook. Once the rice is cooked and drained, set it aside to cool. Place the cooled rice into a bowl and mix in the sweetcorn, beans, spring onions (scallions) red pepper (bell pepper), lime juice and chilli (if using). Combine all of the ingredients well. Season with salt and pepper.

Cooked Ham & Hummus Rolls

179
calories
per serving

Ingredients

3 slices cooked ham
3 tablespoons hummus
2 large handfuls of mixed lettuce leaves

Method

Lay out the slices of ham and spoon hummus at the end of each piece then roll it up. Repeat for the remaining ingredients. Serve on its own or with salad leaves.

Chicken & Avocado Salsa

Ingredients

1 skinless chicken breast

1 teaspoon paprika

1 teaspoon olive oil

FOR THE SALSA:

1 small avocado, peeled and diced

1 tomato, de-seeded and chopped

1 spring onions (scallion) finely chopped

Pinch of chilli flakes

1 teaspoon fresh coriander (cilantro) leaves

Juice of 1 lime

SERVES 1

442
calories
per serving

Method

Place the chicken in a bowl with the oil and paprika and coat it well. Lay it under a hot grill (broiler) and cook for around 6 minutes on each side until cooked through. In the meantime, combine the ingredients for the salsa in a bowl and mix well. Serve the chicken with the salsa on the side. Enjoy.

Grilled Cheddar & Herb Crisps

SERVES 1

313 calories per serving

Ingredients

75g (3oz) Cheddar cheese, grated (shredded)

Sprinkling dried mixed herbs

Method

Place small separate circular amounts of cheese on a baking sheet and sprinkle with a pinch of herbs. Place them under a hot grill (broiler) and melt the cheese until it is bubbling. Allow them to cool. Serve on their own or with dips. Enjoy.

King Prawn Wraps

Ingredients

6 peeled and cooked king prawns
2 tablespoons coleslaw
6 Romaine or iceberg lettuce leaves

SERVES 1

215
calories
per serving

Method

Place the prawns on a serving plate alongside a side dish of coleslaw. Take a lettuce leaf and place a prawn in the middle. Add a dollop of coleslaw and fold over the lettuce leaf. Repeat for the remaining ingredients. Eat straight away

Cheese & Tuna Wraps

Ingredients

- 6 romaine or iceberg lettuce leaves
- 100g (3½ oz) tinned tuna in brine
- 50g (2oz) Cheddar cheese, grated (shredded)
- ¼ cucumber, thinly sliced
- Sprinkling of paprika

SERVES 1

346 calories per serving

Method

Place the tuna, cheese and paprika in a bowl and mix well. Take a lettuce leaf and line it with cucumber slices. Spoon some tune/cheese mixture on top and repeat for the remaining ingredients. Eat straight away.

Pepperoni Bites

Ingredients

8 slices of pepperoni
25g (1oz) Cheddar cheese,
grated (shredded)

SERVES 1

226
calories
per serving

Method

Place the pepperoni slices into a frying pan and add a pinch of cheese into the middle of each slice. Warm the pepperoni until the cheese begins to melt. Serve and eat immediately.

Leek & Butterbean Soup

Ingredients

75g (3oz) tinned cooked butter beans
1 small leek, chopped
1 small carrot, peeled and chopped
300mls vegetable stock (broth)
1 tablespoon olive oil
Sea salt
Freshly ground black pepper

**SERVES
1**

232
calories
per serving

Method

Heat the oil in a saucepan, add the leek and carrot and cook for 3 minutes. Pour in the stock (broth) and add the butter beans. Bring it to the boil and simmer for 20 minutes. You can add additional water or stock (broth) if you need more liquid. Season with salt and pepper.

Speedy Tomato Soup

Ingredients

200g (7oz) tinned chopped tomatoes
1 teaspoon butter
1 spring onion (scallion) chopped
200mls (½ pint) vegetable stock (broth)
1 tablespoon crème fraîche
Sea salt
Freshly ground black pepper

**SERVES
1**

99
calories
per serving

Method

Heat the butter in a saucepan, add the spring onion (scallion) and cook for 5 minutes.
Add in the tomatoes and stock (broth) and bring it to the boil. Reduce the heat and
simmer for 5 minutes. Using a food processor and or hand blender blitz until smooth.
Pour in the crème fraîche and return the soup to the heat until hot. Season with salt
and pepper. Serve and eat straight away.

Cream of Cauliflower Soup

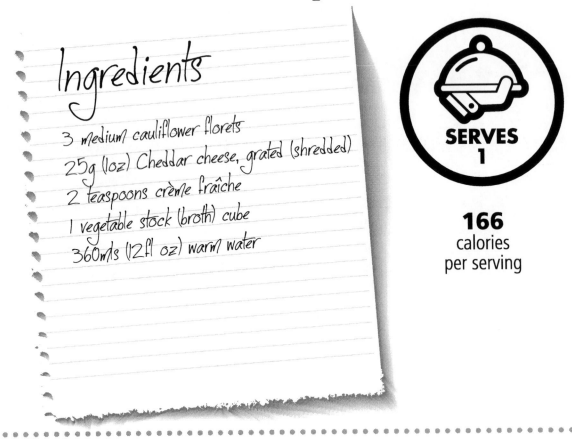

Ingredients

3 medium cauliflower florets

25g (1oz) Cheddar cheese, grated (shredded)

2 teaspoons crème fraîche

1 vegetable stock (broth) cube

360mls (12fl oz) warm water

SERVES 1

166
calories
per serving

Method

Pour the water into a saucepan, add the cauliflower and cook for around 8-10 minutes or until the cauliflower has softened. Add in the stock (broth) cube and stir until it dissolves. Using a hand blender or food processor, whizz the soup until smooth. Add the crème fraîche and stir well. Serve the soup into a bowl and sprinkle with cheese. Enjoy.

Lemon & Courgette Soup

Ingredients

25g (1oz) rice
1 small courgettes (zucchinis), grated (shredded)
1 tablespoon fresh parsley, chopped
2 spring onions, (scallions), chopped
1 clove garlic, chopped
250mls (8fl oz) vegetable stock (broth)
Zest and juice of 1/2 lemon
Sea salt
Freshly ground black pepper

**SERVES
1**

78
calories
per serving

Method

Place the stock (broth,) spring onion (scallion), rice, garlic and parsley into a pan and bring it to the boil. Reduce the heat and simmer for 20 minutes. Stir in the courgettes (zucchinis) and cook for 5 minutes. Add in the lemon zest and juice, salt and pepper. Serve and enjoy.

Cream of Celery Soup

Ingredients

- 1 clove of garlic, chopped
- 3 stalks of celery, chopped
- 1 small onion, chopped
- 25mls (1fl oz) double cream (heavy cream)
- 250mls (8fl oz) vegetable stock (broth)
- 1 teaspoon butter

**SERVES
1**

198
calories
per serving

Method

Heat the butter in a saucepan, add the onion, celery and garlic and cook for 5 minutes until the vegetables have softened. Add in the vegetable stock (broth), bring it to the boil, reduce the heat and simmer for 15 minutes. Stir in the parsley and double cream (heavy cream). Using a food processor or hand blender process the soup until smooth and creamy. Serve and enjoy. If you prefer to make a large batch of soup and store or freeze the leftovers just multiply the quantity to suit you.

Lemon Lentil Salad

Ingredients

75g (1oz) tinned cooked Puy lentils

1 egg, hard boiled, quartered

1 medium tomato, deseeded and chopped

2 spring onions (scallions), finely chopped

1 tablespoon olive oil

1 tablespoon parsley

1 large handful of washed spinach leaves

1 clove of garlic, finely chopped

Juice and rind of 1 lemon

Sea salt

Freshly ground black pepper

**SERVES
1**

328
calories
per serving

Method

Heat the olive oil in a saucepan, add the garlic and spring onions (scallions) and cook for
1 minute. Add the tomatoes, lentils, lemon juice and rind. Cook for 2 minutes. Scatter
the spinach leaves onto plates, serve the lentils on top and add the egg quarters. Season
with salt and pepper.

French Tomato & Roquefort Salad

Ingredients

- 75g (3oz) cherry tomatoes, cut in half
- 50g (2oz) bacon lardons
- 25g (1oz) Roquefort cheese, chopped
- 4 walnut halves, chopped
- 1 clove of garlic, chopped
- 1 handful of spinach leaves
- 1 small bunch basil
- 1 tablespoon red wine vinegar
- 1 teaspoon olive oil
- 1 tablespoon olive oil

**SERVES
1**

539
calories
per serving

Method

Scatter the tomatoes and garlic in an ovenproof dish with a teaspoon of olive oil. Transfer it to the oven and cook at 190C/375F and cook for 15 minutes. In the meantime, cook the lardons in a frying pan for around 4 minutes, remove them and keep them warm. Place the spinach and basil in a large bowl. Heat a tablespoon of olive oil and the red wine vinegar in the frying pan until just slightly warm. Pour the oil/vinegar over the spinach and basil. Add the tomatoes, garlic and bacon to the salad and toss the salad. Scatter the Roquefort and walnuts into the salad. Serve and eat straight away.

Warm Chorizo & Beetroot Salad

Ingredients

100g (3½ oz) cooked Puy lentils
75g (3oz) beetroot (unsweetened), chopped
50g (2oz) chorizo sausage, chopped
1 handful of mixed salad leaves
1 small onion, peeled and finely chopped
2 teaspoons olive oil
1 teaspoon red wine vinegar

**SERVES
1**

388
calories
per serving

Method

Heat the oil in a large frying pan, add the onion and cook until softened. Add in the chorizo and cook for 2 minutes. Add in the beetroot, vinegar and lentils and warm the ingredients through. Scatter the salad leaves on a plate and serve the chorizo mixture on top. Serve and eat straight away.

Feta & Broad Bean Salad

Ingredients

100g (3½ oz) broad beans

75g (3oz) feta cheese, crumbled or diced

1 large handful of rocket (arugula) leaves

2 teaspoons olive oil

1 tablespoon lemon juice

Sea salt

Freshly ground black pepper

SERVES 1

322 calories per serving

Method

Cook the beans in boiling water for around 3 minutes until they are tender. Drain them, dip them in cool water then set aside and make sure they are properly drained. Combine the feta cheese in a bowl with the rocket (arugula) leaves and cold broad beans. Pour on the olive oil and squeeze on the lemon juice. Season with salt and pepper. Chill and serve.

Roast Pepper & Feta Salad

Ingredients

50g (2oz) feta cheese, crumbled
1 red peppers (bell pepper), halved and de-seeded
1 tablespoons olive oil
Sea salt
Freshly ground black pepper

SERVES 1

282
calories
per serving

Method

Place the pepper under a hot grill (broiler) until the skin begins to blacken. Remove them and place them inside a plastic bag for several minutes to help loosen the skin. Peel off skin and transfer the peppers to a serving plate. Chop the pepper and place it in a bowl with the oil and feta cheese and mix well. Season with salt and pepper.

Smoked Salmon Salad

Ingredients

1 small carrot, peeled and grated (shredded)
2 radishes, chopped
1 tablespoon cream cheese
3 slices smoked salmon
5cm (2 inch) cucumber, chopped
Juice of ½ lemon
Small bunch of fresh basil leaves
1 teaspoon olive oil (optional)
Freshly ground black pepper

**SERVES
1**

226
calories
per serving

Method

Place the vegetables in a bowl and squeeze in the lemon juice and a sprinkle of black pepper.
Stir in the cream cheese and combine the ingredients well. Serve the mixture onto a plate and
lay the salmon slices on top of the vegetables. Drizzle with a little olive oil (if using).

Orange & Kale Salad

Ingredients

100g (3 ½ oz) kale, washed and finely chopped

1 orange, peeled, segmented and chopped

1 tablespoon roasted pistachio nuts

Juice of ½ lemon

1 tablespoon olive oil

SERVES 1

365
calories
per serving

Method

Place the kale in a bowl and add in the lemon juice, olive oil and mix well then allow it to stand for 5 minutes. Add in the chopped orange and pistachio nuts and serve.

Feta & Watermelon Salad

Ingredients

150g (5oz) watermelon, skin removed and cut into thick chunks
50g (2oz) feta cheese, crumbled
1 shallot, finely chopped
Several mint leaves, finely chopped
Freshly ground black pepper

SERVES 1

176
calories
per serving

Method

Place the watermelon, shallot, feta and mint leaves in a bowl and mix to combine all of the ingredients together. Season with a little black pepper and serve.

Avocado Baked Eggs

Ingredients

2 small eggs
1 avocado, halved and stones removed
1 teaspoon fresh parsley, chopped

SERVES 1

384
calories
per serving

Method

Place each avocado half in a ramekin dish with the hollow facing upwards. Crack an egg into the each avocado half. You may need to remove a little avocado flesh to get the whole egg in if it is particularly large. Sprinkle with parsley. Bake in an oven, preheated to 220C/440F and cook for 20 minutes, or until the eggs have set. Serve and enjoy!

Grilled Cheddar Courgette

Ingredients

50g (2oz) Cheddar cheese, grated (shredded)

1 courgettes (zucchinis), sliced into 2cm (1 inch) pieces

1 teaspoon olive oil

1 teaspoon fresh parsley

SERVES 1

278 calories per serving

Method

Heat the oil in a frying pan. Add the courgette (zucchini) and cook until it softens. Transfer the courgette slices to a baking sheet and sprinkle over the cheese and parsley. Place under a hot grill (broiler) for 3-4 minutes until the cheese melts. Serve straight away.

Dinner

King Prawn Satay

Ingredients

- 10 king prawns (shrimps), peeled and de-veined
- 10 button mushrooms
- 1/2 teaspoon tamari sauce
- 1 tablespoon smooth peanut butter
- 1 teaspoon curry powder
- 100ml (3½ fl oz) coconut milk
- Juice of ½ lemon
- Dash of Tabasco sauce

**SERVES
1**

447
calories
per serving

Method

Preheat the oven to 200C/400F. In a bowl, combine the peanut butter and coconut milk. Stir in the curry powder, Tabasco and tamari sauce. Coat the prawns in the peanut sauce. Thread the prawns (shrimps) onto skewers, alternating with the mushrooms. Set aside the remaining satay sauce. Place the skewers under a hot grill (broiler) and cook for 3-4 minutes on each side, making sure the prawns completely pink throughout. Pour the remaining satay sauce into a saucepan along with lemon juice and bring it to the boil. Serve the chicken skewers and spoon the warm satay sauce over the top.

Piri Piri Chicken

Ingredients

- 1 large handful mixed salad leaves
- 1 large chicken breast
- 1 red pepper (bell pepper), roughly chopped
- 1 small red chilli, de-seeded
- 1 tablespoon red wine vinegar
- 1 tablespoon olive oil
- 1 teaspoon olive oil

**SERVES
1**

473
calories
per serving

Method

Place the red pepper (bell pepper), a teaspoon of oil, vinegar and chilli into a blender and process lightly until the mixture is roughly chopped. Spoon the mixture onto the chicken and marinate for 20 minutes or longer if you can. Heat a tablespoon of olive oil in a pan, add the chicken and cook for 6 minutes on each side. Serve with mixed salad leaves.

Almond & Lemon Baked Cod

**SERVES
1**

343
calories
per serving

Ingredients

2 teaspoons butter

1 tablespoon ground almonds (almond meal/
almond flour)

1 large cod fillet

½ teaspoon sea salt

½ teaspoon white pepper

Zest and juice of ½ lemon

Method

Heat the butter in a saucepan, add the lemon zest and rind then set it aside. On a large plate, combine the ground almonds (almond meal/almond flour), salt and pepper. Dip the fish in the lemon butter mixture then dip it in the almond mixture, coating it completely. Place the fish in an ovenproof dish. Transfer it to the oven and cook at 180C/360F for around 25 minutes, or until the fish is flaky. Serve with a wedge of lemon and heaps of green salad.

Orange & Sesame Chicken Stir- Fry

Ingredients

75g (3oz) broccoli, broken into florets

75g (3oz) baby corn

1 tablespoon unsalted peanuts, chopped

1 chicken breast, sliced

1/2 red pepper (bell pepper), chopped

1 teaspoon toasted sesame seeds

1 teaspoon cornflour (cornstarch)

2 teaspoons soy sauce

3 tablespoons fresh unsweetened orange juice

2 teaspoons olive oil

1 teaspoon sesame oil

**SERVES
1**

484
calories
per serving

Method

Heat both of the oils in a large frying pan. Add the chicken and cook for 4-5 minutes. Add in the broccoli, red pepper (bell pepper) and baby corn. Stir and cook for 2 minutes. In a separate bowl, combine the soy sauce, orange juice and cornflour. Pour it into the saucepan with the chicken and vegetables. The sauce will thicken and form a glaze. Sprinkle on the peanuts and sesame seeds and warm them through.

Chilli Bean Bake

Ingredients

- 200g (7oz) tinned chopped tomatoes
- 125g (4oz) haricot beans
- 50g (2 oz) peas
- 25g (1oz) rolled oats
- 25g (1oz) Cheddar cheese, grated (shredded)
- 1 handful spinach leaves
- 1 clove of garlic, crushed
- 1 small onion, chopped
- 2 teaspoons olive oil
- 2 teaspoons soy sauce
- 1/4 teaspoon chilli flakes
- 1/4 teaspoon dried oregano

SERVES 1

498 calories per serving

Method

Heat the olive oil in a frying pan, add the garlic, onion, chilli and oregano. Cook for 4 minutes. Stir in the chopped tomatoes, oats and beans and cook for 5 minutes. Stir in the peas, spinach and soy sauce. Transfer the mixture to an ovenproof dish and sprinkle with cheese. Bake in the oven at 200C/400F for 10 minutes until the cheese is bubbling.

Fresh Salmon & Rice Salad

Ingredients

50g (2oz) brown basmati rice
1 salmon fillet (approx. 100g)
1 red chilli pepper, de-seeded and chopped
1/4 cucumber, diced
3 spring onions (scallions), finely chopped
1 small handful of coriander (cilantro) leaves, chopped
2 teaspoons soy sauce
1 tablespoon lemon juice

SERVES 1

495 calories per serving

Method

Boil the rice according to the instructions the set aside. Grill the salmon fillet for 10-15 minutes until cooked through, turning once half way through. Remove the salmon skin and flake the fish through the rice. Combine the rice mixture with the cucumber, spring onions (scallions), coriander (cilantro), lemon juice and soy sauce. Serve and enjoy.

Spiced Coriander Chicken

Ingredients

1 chicken breast
1 small onion, finely chopped
1 clove of garlic, crushed
1 lemon, sliced and pips removed
1/4 teaspoon ground coriander
1/4 teaspoon ground ginger
1/4 teaspoon ground cumin
1/4 teaspoon ground turmeric
1 teaspoon olive oil
100mls (3½ fl oz) chicken stock (broth)
15g (½ oz) pitted green olives, in brine
1 small bunch fresh coriander (cilantro) finely chopped

**SERVES
1**

281
calories
per serving

Method

Heat the oil in a saucepan, add the onion and cook for around 5 minutes or until softened. Add the garlic, cumin, turmeric, ginger and ground coriander (cilantro) and cook for 1 minute. Add the chicken and brown it. Add the slices of lemon and chicken stock (broth). Bring it to the boil, reduce the heat and simmer for 30 minutes. Stir in the fresh coriander (cilantro) and olives. Warm it through and serve.

Creole Chicken

Ingredients

200g (7oz) tinned chopped tomatoes
75g (3oz) mangetout (snow peas)
1 chicken breast
1 clove garlic, chopped
1 teaspoon curry powder
1/2 teaspoon ground cumin
1/4 teaspoon paprika
50mls (2fl oz) chicken stock (broth)
1 teaspoon olive oil

**SERVES
1**

265
calories
per serving

Method

Heat the oil in a frying pan, add the chicken, cumin, paprika and curry powder and cook for 3 minutes, stirring frequently. Add the garlic, tomatoes and stock (broth). Bring it to the boil then reduce the heat and simmer for 15 minutes. Stir in the mangetout (snow peas) and cook for 10 minutes. Serve with brown rice.

Fresh Monkfish With Parsley & Garlic Butter

Ingredients

150g (5oz) monkfish, cut into chunks
1 tablespoon butter
1 cloves of garlic, finely chopped or crushed
1 teaspoon fresh parsley, chopped
1 large handful fresh spinach leaves

SERVES 1

266 calories per serving

Method

Heat the butter in a frying pan, add the garlic and sauté for 1 minute. Add the monkfish and cook for around 2-3 minutes on either side. To check if it's cooked, insert a knife into the fish and if it comes out hot the fish is cooked through. Serve the spinach leaves onto a plate and serve the monkfish on top. Sprinkle with parsley. Eat straight away.

Pesto Chicken & Courgette 'Spaghetti'

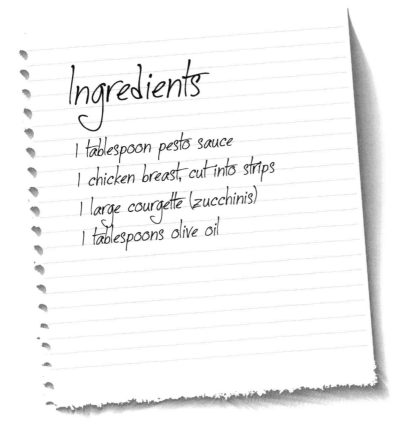

Ingredients

- 1 tablespoon pesto sauce
- 1 chicken breast, cut into strips
- 1 large courgette (zucchinis)
- 1 tablespoons olive oil

SERVES 1

396 calories per serving

Method

Place the chicken strips into a bowl and add the pesto sauce. Coat the chicken well in the pesto. Heat the olive oil in a frying pan, add the chicken and cook for 5-6 minutes or until the chicken is completely cooked. Remove the chicken and keep it warm. In the meantime, using a spiraliser cut the courgette (zucchini) into long strips. If you don't have a spiraliser use a vegetable peeler and peel thin strips off the courgette (zucchini), cutting them in half with a knife if they are too thick. Place the courgette strips into the pan and cook for 2-3 minutes until soft. Serve the courgette spaghetti onto plates and place the chicken on top.

Coconut & Chilli Salmon

Ingredients

- 1 head of pak choi (bok choy), roughly chopped
- 1 salmon fillet
- 50mls (2fl oz) coconut milk
- 1 small bunch of coriander (cilantro) leaves
- ½ teaspoon ground ginger
- ½ teaspoon garam masala
- 1 clove of garlic, crushed
- Pinch of chilli flakes

SERVES 1

382 calories per serving

Method

Pour the coconut milk into a blender and add in the ginger, garam masala, garlic, chilli and coriander (cilantro). Process until smooth. Scatter the pak choi (bok choy) in an ovenproof dish. Place the salmon on top and pour the coconut milk over the fish. Transfer it to the oven and bake at 220C/440F for 15-20 minutes until the fish is cooked through. Serve and eat straight away.

Roast Chicken, Bacon & Leeks

SERVES 1

427
calories
per serving

Ingredients

1 large skinless chicken breast
1 leek, roughly chopped
2 slices of bacon
1 teaspoon olive oil
A few thyme leaves
Sea salt
Freshly ground black pepper

Method

Place the chopped leek, oil, thyme and olive oil into a bowl and mix well. Transfer the leek mixture to an ovenproof dish. Wrap both of the bacon slices around the chicken breast and place it on top of the leeks. Season with salt and pepper. Transfer the dish to the oven, preheated to 200C/400F and cook for around 30 minutes or until the chicken is completely cooked. Serve and enjoy.

Speedy Vegetable Curry

Ingredients

100g (3½ oz) frozen mixed vegetables

200g (7oz) tinned chopped tomatoes

1 clove of garlic, chopped

1 tablespoon tomato purée (paste)

2 teaspoons curry powder

1 small onion, chopped

100mls (1½ oz) vegetable stock (broth)

1 tablespoon olive oil

1 small handful coriander (cilantro) chopped

**SERVES
1**

260
calories
per serving

Method

Heat the oil in a saucepan. Add the onion and garlic and cook until softened. Stir in the tomato purée (paste) and curry powder and cook for 2 minutes. Add in the vegetables, tomatoes and stock (broth). Cook for around 20 minutes, or until the vegetables are cooked through. Stir in the coriander (cilantro) leaves and serve with brown rice or a baked potato.

Crab Linguine

Ingredients

100g (3½ oz) linguine
2 teaspoons olive oil
2 garlic cloves, finely sliced
1 tablespoon crème fraîche
100g (3½ oz) white crab meat
1 small handful of spinach leaves
Zest of ½ lemon
Freshly ground black pepper

**SERVES
1**

427
calories
per serving

Method

Cook the linguine according to the instructions on the package. Heat the olive oil in a frying pan and add the garlic. Cook for around 30 seconds then stir in the crab meat, crème fraîche, lemon and spinach and warm the ingredients completely. Once the linguine has cooked, add it to the pan and stir to coat it well. Season with black pepper. Serve onto a plate and enjoy.

Chorizo & Tomato Hash

Ingredients

100g (3½ oz) cooked potatoes, diced (leftovers are perfect)

75g (3oz) cherry tomatoes

50g (2oz) chorizo sausage, chopped

1 small onion, sliced

½ red pepper (bell pepper), chopped

1 tablespoons fresh parsley, chopped

½ teaspoon paprika

1 tablespoons olive oil

SERVES 1

450 calories per serving

Method

Heat the olive oil in a frying pan. Add the onion and peppers and cook for 5 minutes. Add in the chorizo, potatoes, paprika and tomatoes and warm them thoroughly Sprinkle with parsley and serve.

Quick Beef Stroganoff

Ingredients

100g (3½ oz) beef, cut into strips
50g (2oz) rice
50g (2oz) mushrooms, sliced
1 teaspoon paprika
1 teaspoon plain flour (all-purpose flour)
1 shallot, peeled and chopped
50mls (2fl oz) sour cream
2 teaspoons olive oil
Sea salt
Freshly ground black pepper
1 teaspoon fresh parsley, chopped

**SERVES
1**

588
calories
per serving

Method

Cook the rice according to the instructions on the label. In the meantime, place the beef in a bowl and coat it in the flour and paprika. Heat the oil in a frying pan, add the shallot and cook for 5 minutes. Add in the mushrooms and cook until they soften. Add the beef to the frying pan and cook until browned. Stir the sour cream into the pan and still well until the cream is bubbling. Season with salt and pepper. Serve the rice and spoon the stroganoff over the top and add a sprinkle of parsley.

Turkey & Cannellini One Pot

SERVES 1

363
calories
per serving

Ingredients

100g (3½ oz) cannellini beans, drained

1 large tomato, chopped

1 turkey steak

1 tablespoons fresh parsley, chopped

1 red pepper (bell peppers)

1 small onion, chopped

1 teaspoon red wine vinegar

1 teaspoon olive oil

Sea salt

Freshly ground black pepper

Method

Heat the olive oil in a frying pan, add the turkey and cook for around 3-4 minutes on each side until cooked through. Remove them, set aside and keep them warm. Add the pepper (bell pepper), tomato and onion to the pan and cook for 5 minutes until the vegetables have softened. Add the parsley, vinegar and cannellini beans and warm it through. Season with salt and pepper. Warm the turkey steak if necessary. Serve the turkey and spoon the vegetables over the top. Enjoy.

Chilli & Lime Lamb Chops

Ingredients

- 3 loin lamb chops
- 1 large handful of mixed salad leaves
- 2 spring onions (scallions), chopped

FOR THE MARINADE:
- Juice of 1 lime
- 2 tablespoons fresh coriander (cilantro), chopped
- 1 clove of garlic
- 1 tablespoon olive oil
- 1 red chilli

SERVES 1

312 calories per serving

Method

Place all the ingredients for the marinade into a blender and blitz until smooth. Transfer half of the marinade to a separate bowl to be used as a dressing after cooking. Put the lamb onto a plate and pour the other half of the dressing over the lamb. Marinate for 30 minutes or longer if you can. Grill the lamb chops for around 4 minutes on each side. Longer if you like them well cooked. Scatter the salad leaves and spring onions (scallions) on a plate. Serve the chops onto plates and spoon over the dressing.

Mini Cod Gratin

Ingredients

- 25g (1oz) Gruyère cheese, grated (shredded)
- 4 peeled, cooked king prawns (shrimps)
- 1 tomato, chopped
- 1 skinless cod fillet, chopped
- 1 teaspoon Parmesan cheese, grated (shredded)
- ½ teaspoon butter
- 1 small bunch of chives, chopped
- 25mls (1fl oz) double cream (heavy cream)
- Sea salt
- Freshly ground black pepper

**SERVES
1**

404
calories
per serving

Method

Grease a small ovenproof dish with butter. Scatter the tomato, chives, cod and prawns in the dish. Pour the cream into the dish and add the cheese on top. Season with salt and pepper. Transfer it to the oven, preheated to 220C/440F and cook for around 20 minutes or until the fish is completely cooked. Serve with salad or mashed potatoes and vegetables. You can easily multiply the quantities in the recipe to make extra gratins which can be frozen and stored.

Sausage Casserole

Ingredients

100g (5oz) tinned cannellini beans, chopped

75g (3oz) good quality sausage, cut into chunks

50g (2oz) passata sauce or tinned tomatoes

1 red pepper (bell pepper)

1 small onion, peeled and finely chopped

1 clove of garlic, chopped

1 tablespoon fresh oregano, chopped

1 teaspoon olive oil

Sea salt

Freshly ground black pepper

SERVES 1

437 calories per serving

Method

Heat olive oil in a large saucepan, add the sausage and cook for 2 minutes. Add in the onion, red pepper (bell pepper) and garlic and cook for 5 minutes. Pour in the passata/tomatoes, beans and oregano. Cook for 15-20 minutes. Season with salt and pepper. Serve and enjoy. As a variation on this recipe you can try using Italian or Spanish for a Mediterranean flavour.

Tomato & Mozzarella Chicken

**SERVES
1**

500
calories
per serving

Ingredients

- 100g (3½ oz) passata (or tinned chopped tomatoes)
- 25g (1oz) Parmesan cheese, grated (shredded)
- 25g (1oz) mozzarella cheese, grated (shredded)
- 1 chicken breast
- 1 small egg
- 1 tablespoon ground almonds (almond meal/almond flour)
- 1 teaspoon fresh oregano
- Salt and black pepper
- A few fresh basil leaves

Method

Place the ground almonds (almond meal/almond flour) in a bowl and mix in the Parmesan cheese, oregano, salt and pepper. In a separate bowl, whisk the egg. Pour the passata/tomatoes into a small ovenproof dish. Dip the chicken breast in the egg then dunk it in the almond mixture. Lay the chicken on top of the tomato base. Place a few basil leaves on top of the chicken and cover the chicken with the mozzarella cheese. Transfer the dish to the oven, preheated to 220C/440F for around 25-30 minutes or until the chicken is completely cooked. Serve with a heap of salad leaves on the side. Enjoy.

Beef, Green Pepper & Black Beans

Ingredients

1 clove of garlic, chopped
½ teaspoon ground ginger
1 tablespoon black beans
1 small onion, chopped
½ green pepper (bell pepper), chopped
1 teaspoon olive oil
½ teaspoon cornflour (mix with a teaspoon of water to make a paste)

FOR THE MARINATED BEEF:
125g (4oz) steak, cut into strips
2 teaspoons soy sauce
1 teaspoon sesame oil
Salt and pepper

**SERVES
1**

384
calories
per serving

Method

Combine the beef with the soy sauce, sesame oil, salt and pepper and marinade for at least 20 minutes. Mix together the ginger, garlic, and black beans with the olive oil then set aside. Heat a frying pan or wok. Add the meat and stir-fry for 3-4 minutes. Remove the meat and keep it warm. Put the green pepper (bell pepper) and onion into the pan. Cook for 3 minutes then return the beef to the pan. Add in the ginger, garlic and black beans and cook for 2-3 minutes. Remove from the heat and stir in the cornflour paste. Stir until it thickens. Serve with rice and baby corn and enjoy.

Apple & Mustard Pork

Ingredients

1 medium pork steak
1 teaspoon olive oil
1 small onion, chopped
Sea salt
Freshly ground black pepper to taste
1 apple, peeled cored and thickly sliced
1/4 teaspoon mustard
25mls (1fl oz) hot water

SERVES 1

269 calories per serving

Method

Heat the oil in a frying pan, add the onion and cook for 2 minutes. Add the pork and brown it on both sides. Transfer the pork and onion to a small ovenproof dish. Spread the mustard on the pork and season with salt and pepper. Add the hot water and apple slices to the dish. Place it in the oven, preheated to 190C/375F and cook for around 35 minutes or until the pork is completely cooked. Serve with a leafy green salad or roast vegetables.

Roast Chicken, Mushroom & Asparagus

Ingredients

- 6 asparagus spears
- 8 button mushrooms
- 4 cherry tomatoes
- 1 chicken breast, skin on
- 1/2 teaspoon paprika
- 1/4 teaspoon dried mixed herbs
- 2 teaspoons olive oil
- Sea salt
- Freshly ground black pepper

SERVES 1

298 calories per serving

Method

Scatter the asparagus, mushrooms and tomatoes in an ovenproof dish. Sprinkle the mixed herbs over the vegetables. Place the chicken in a bowl and sprinkle it with paprika, making sure both sides are well coated. Transfer the chicken to the ovenproof dish and pour the olive oil over the chicken and vegetables. Season with salt and pepper. Transfer it to the oven, preheated to 200C/400F and cook for around 30 minutes.

Vegetable Quinoa

Ingredients

- 200g (7oz) tinned black beans
- 50g (2oz) frozen peas
- 50g (2oz) quinoa
- 2 spring onions (scallions) chopped
- 2 cloves garlic, chopped
- 1 teaspoon ground cumin
- 1 vegetable stock (broth) cube
- 1 tablespoon fresh coriander (cilantro) chopped
- 1/4 teaspoon sea salt
- 1/4 teaspoon cayenne pepper
- 1 teaspoon olive oil

SERVES 1

465 calories per serving

Method

Place the quinoa in a saucepan and cover it with boiling water. Add the stock (broth) cube, cumin, cayenne pepper and salt. Bring it to the boil, reduce the heat and cook for 15-20 minutes or until the grains are soft. Drain it and set it aside. Heat the oil in a saucepan, add the spring onions (scallions) and garlic and cook for 2 minutes. Add in the black beans and frozen peas and cook until warmed through. Stir in the coriander (cilantro) and serve.

Roast Prawns & Broccoli

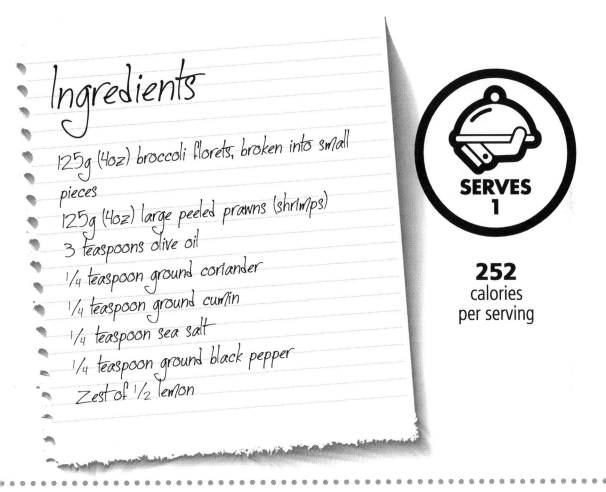

Ingredients

- 125g (4oz) broccoli florets, broken into small pieces
- 125g (4oz) large peeled prawns (shrimps)
- 3 teaspoons olive oil
- 1/4 teaspoon ground coriander
- 1/4 teaspoon ground cumin
- 1/4 teaspoon sea salt
- 1/4 teaspoon ground black pepper
- Zest of 1/2 lemon

SERVES 1

252 calories per serving

Method

Place the prawns (shrimps) into a bowl with a teaspoon of olive oil and the lemon zest and coat them in the mixture. In a separate bowl, place the broccoli in a bowl with two teaspoons of olive oil, cumin, coriander (cilantro), salt and pepper and coat the broccoli in the seasoning. Scatter the broccoli on a baking tray, transfer it to the oven, preheated to 220C/425F and cook for 8-10 minutes. Remove the baking tray and add the prawns, tossing them in the broccoli and oil mixture. Return it to the oven and continue cooking for 10 minutes making sure the prawns are completely cooked and opaque.

Quinoa & Spinach Pilaf

Ingredients

50g (2oz) quinoa
25g (1oz) Cheddar cheese, grated (shredded)
1 large handful of spinach leaves
1 tablespoon pine nuts
1 clove of garlic
1 tablespoon olive oil
1 tablespoon lemon juice

**SERVES
1**

454
calories
per serving

Method

Heat a saucepan of lightly salted water to the boil. Add the quinoa and cook for around 15 minutes or until it is soft and tender. Drain it and set aside. Heat the olive oil in a frying pan, add the pine nuts and garlic and cook for 2 minutes. Add the spinach and cook for 1 minute. Add in the quinoa and cook until warmed through. Add the lemon juice and cheese and mix well. Serve and eat immediately.

Pork Kebabs & Roast Pepper Salad

Ingredients

125g (4oz) pork mince (ground pork)
1 red pepper (bell peppers), halved and deseeded
1 large handful of lettuce leaves
1 teaspoon ground cumin
1 teaspoon ground coriander
1 small onion, finely chopped
1 egg white
1/4 teaspoon cayenne pepper
1 handful of fresh parsley, chopped
1 tablespoon olive oil

FOR THE DIP:
50g (2oz) Greek yogurt
1 tablespoon fresh parsley, chopped
1 tablespoon lemon juice

SERVES 1

472
calories
per serving

Method

Place the pepper under a hot grill (broiler) and cook until the skin is charred. Place the pepper into a plastic bag and seal for a few minutes until the skin loosens them peel it off. Chop the pepper and set aside. Heat the olive oil in a pan, add the onion and cook until softened. Stir in the spices and cook for 2 minutes. In a bowl, combine the onion, pork, egg white and parsley. Make the mixture into 2 shapes and slide them onto 2 skewers. Place the skewers under a hot grill (broiler) and cook for about 8 minutes, turning occasionally until completely cooked. In a bowl, combine the ingredients for the dip. Serve the lettuce leaves and chopped peppers onto plates. Add the cooked kebabs and serve with the dip.

Sweets, Desserts & Snacks

Raspberry Crumble

Ingredients

125g (4oz) raspberries

25g (2oz) ground almonds (almond meal/almond flour)

25g (1oz) desiccated (shredded) coconut

1 teaspoon coconut oil

½ teaspoon stevia powder, or to taste (optional)

Zest of 1 lemon

SERVES 1

384 calories each

Method

Place the ground almonds (almond meal/almond flour), coconut and lemon zest in a bowl and mix together. Warm the coconut oil and stevia and pour it into the almond mixture. Mix it well. Put the raspberries and into a small ovenproof dish. Cover them with the almond and coconut mixture. Bake in the oven at 180C/350F for 15 minutes until the top becomes slightly golden. Serve on its own or with a dollop of crème fraîche or cream.

Strawberry & Cream Scones

Ingredients

75g (3oz) self-raising flour
25g (1oz) butter
1 teaspoon stevia sweetener
75mls (3fl oz) milk

FOR THE TOPPING:
75g (3oz) fresh ripe strawberries, chopped
75mls (3fl oz) double cream (heavy cream)

MAKES 4

284 calories each

Method

Place the flour and stevia in a bowl and stir. Cut flakes of butter into the flour and using clean hands, rub it into the flour. Pour in the milk and mix to a dough. Grease and line a baking sheet. Scatter some flour onto a work surface and roll out the scone mixture to 2cm (1 inch) thick. Use a cookie cutter and cut into rounds. Place them onto the baking sheet and coat them with some extra milk. Transfer them to the oven, preheated to 180C/360F for around 20 minutes or until golden. Allow them to cool. Whisk the double cream (heavy cream) until thick. When ready to serve, cut the scones in half, dollop some cream on top and scatter chopped strawberries onto the cream. Enjoy!

Chocolate Mousse

Ingredients

50mls (2fl oz) crème fraîche
50g (2oz) cream cheese
2 teaspoons 100% cocoa powder
1 teaspoon stevia (or to taste)

**SERVES
1**

248
calories
per serving

Method

Place the stevia and cream cheese into a bowl and mix until smooth. Stir in the cocoa powder and mix thoroughly. Whip the crème fraîche until thick and fold it into cheese mixture. Spoon the mousse into a tall glass or serving bowl. Chill before eating.

Chocolate Chia Pudding

Ingredients

25g (1oz) chia seeds
50mls (2fl oz) coconut milk
125mls (4fl oz) water
2 teaspoons 100% cocoa powder
½ - 1 teaspoons stevia sweetener

**SERVES
1**

237
calories
per serving

Method

Place the chia seeds, cocoa powder and stevia into a bowl. Pour in the coconut milk and water and mix really well. Cover it and chill in the fridge for 20 minutes (or prepare and leave it overnight, ready for breakfast) then serve and enjoy.

Strawberry & Lime Mug Cheesecake

SERVES 1

230 calories each

Ingredients

50g (2oz) cream cheese
25g (1oz) strawberries
1 tablespoon crème fraîche
1 egg
1 teaspoon lemon juice
½ teaspoon vanilla extract
½ teaspoon stevia extract (or to taste)

Method

Place all the ingredients, except the strawberries, into a large mug or a microwaveable bowl and mix well. Cook in the microwave for 30 seconds, remove and stir then return it to the microwave for another 30 seconds, remove and stir. Return it to the microwave for another 30 seconds. Chill in the fridge before serving. Serve with a scattering of strawberries.

Cinnamon & Walnut Mug Cake

Ingredients

2 teaspoons ground linseeds (flaxseeds)

25g (1oz) ground almonds (almond meal/almond flour)

3 walnut halves, chopped

1 egg

1/2 teaspoon vanilla extract

1/2 teaspoon baking powder

1/2 teaspoon cinnamon

1/4 teaspoon stevia (or to taste)

1 teaspoon butter

Pinch of salt

SERVES
1

381
calories
per serving

Method

Place all the ingredients, except the walnuts, into a large mug or a microwaveable bowl and mix well. Cook in the microwave for 30 seconds, remove and stir then return it to the microwave for another 30 seconds, remove and stir in the walnuts. Return it to the microwave for another 30 seconds. Chill in the fridge before serving. Serve and enjoy.

Fresh Raspberry Protein Bars

MAKES 12

142 calories per serving

Ingredients

125g (4oz) peanut butter
175g (6oz) oats
75g (3oz) raspberries
50g (2oz) linseeds (flaxseeds)
2 teaspoons stevia

Method

Place the oats, peanut butter, stevia and linseeds (flaxseeds) into a food processor and process until smooth. Stir in the raspberries. Spoon the mixture into a small baking tin and smooth it out. Chill in the fridge for 2 hours until the mixture has set. Cut it into bars and eat straight away or store them in the fridge. You could try substituting the raspberries for blueberries or chopped strawberries and unsweetened chocolate chips.

Passion Fruit & Raspberry Cream Swirl

Ingredients

50g (2oz) mascarpone cheese
50g (2oz) raspberries
Seeds of 1 passion fruit
A few extra raspberries to garnish

SERVES 1

235
calories
per serving

Method

In a large bowl, stir the seeds from the passion fruit into the mascarpone and mix well. Place the raspberries in a separate bowl and mash them to a pulp. Using a tall glass or dessert bowl, spoon a layer of the mascarpone in then add a spoonful of the raspberry purée and swirl it slightly, repeat with another layer of mascarpone and raspberry until the mixture has been used up. Garnish with a few raspberries and chill before serving.

Apple & Almond Flapjacks

Ingredients

75g (3oz) oats

50g (2oz) almond butter (or smooth peanut butter)

50g (2oz) ground almonds (almond flour/ almond meal)

1 large apple, peeled, cored and finely chopped

1 teaspoon ground cinnamon

1/2 teaspoon ground mixed spice

1/2 teaspoon ground nutmeg

1 teaspoon stevia sweetener

3 tablespoons water

MAKES
6

169
calories
each

Method

Place the apples and water into a saucepan and cook until soft, stirring constantly and adding a little extra water if it starts to stick. Remove them and set aside to cool down. Place the oats, ground almonds (almond meal/almond flour) and spices into a bowl and combine them. Place the almond butter and stevia together into a bowl and warm them in the microwave until it has melted. Combine the nut butter mixture with the dry ingredients and mix well. Add in the cooked apple and combine it. Line a small baking tin and spoon the mixture into it, smoothing it down. Cover and chill in the fridge before cutting it into slices.

High Protein Chocolate Biscuits

Ingredients

125g (4oz) tinned chickpeas (garbanzo beans)
50g (2oz) smooth peanut butter
1 1/2 tablespoons 100% cocoa powder
1/2 teaspoon vanilla extract
1/2 teaspoon stevia sweetener
1/2 teaspoon baking powder
100mls (3 1/2 fl oz) almond milk

MAKES approx.8

68 calories each

Method

Place all of the ingredients into a blender and process until smooth and creamy. If the mixture seems too thick try adding a little extra milk. Scoop out a spoonful of the mixture and place it on a greased baking tray. Repeat for the remaining mixture. Place it in the oven, preheated to 200C/400F and cook for 15 minutes. Allow them to cool. Store in an airtight container.

Cookie Dough Bites

Ingredients

100g (3 ½ oz) oats
75g (3oz) almond nut butter
2 teaspoons vanilla extract
1-2 teaspoons stevia (optional)
150mls (5fl oz) almond milk

MAKES 9

99 calories each

Method

Place the oats into a food processor and blitz until they become like flour. Add in the stevia (optional) and mix well. Add the almond butter, vanilla and half of the milk and pulse the mixture in the food processor. Gradually add in the remaining milk until it becomes a dough-like consistency. Grease and line a baking tray. Scoop the mixture into the baking tray and smooth it down. Cover and chill for at least 3 hours. Cut the mixture into small squares. Serve and enjoy. For a variation to this recipe you can add some raw cocoa chips or drizzle with melted dark chocolate.

Lemon Cheese Bites

Ingredients

50g (2oz) finely ground oats
25g (1oz) mascarpone cheese
1 teaspoon stevia powder (or to taste)
Zest and juice of 1/2 lemon
1 teaspoon vegetable oil
1/2 teaspoon vanilla extract

**MAKES
6**

57
calories
each

Method

Place the mascarpone in a bowl with the stevia, lemon zest, lemon juice, vanilla and vegetable oil. Stir in the oats and combine all of the ingredients until it becomes doughy. Scoop out spoonfuls of the mixture, shape them into balls and flatten them on a baking tray. Transfer them to the oven and bake at 170C/325F for 10 minutes. Allow to cool. Serve and enjoy. This recipe makes a small quantity of biscuits, suitable for one person to store however feel free to multiply the quantity to produce a larger batch.

Blueberry Breakfast Muffins

Ingredients

- 100g (3 ½ oz) wholemeal self-raising flour
- 75g (3oz) blueberries
- 25g (1oz) porridge oats
- 1 teaspoons bicarbonate of soda (baking soda)
- 1 teaspoons stevia sweetener (or to taste)
- 1 ripe bananas, mashed
- 1 small egg
- 50mls (2fl oz) milk

MAKES 6

103 calories each

Method

Place the flour, oats, stevia and bicarbonate of soda (baking soda) into a bowl. In a separate bowl, mix together the mashed banana and egg. Add in the milk and mix well. Add the flour mixture into the wet mixture and mix well until there are no bits of flour or oats uncoated. Stir in the blueberries. Spoon the mixture into a 6-hole muffin tin. Transfer them to the oven and bake at 180C/360F for 20 minutes until slightly golden. Test the muffins with a skewer which should come out clean when they are cooked. Set them on a wire rack to cool.

Fresh Apricot Muffins

Ingredients

50g (2oz) coconut flour
50g (2oz) apricots, stone removed and chopped
1 small egg, beaten
1 ripe banana, mashed
2 tablespoons coconut oil, melted
1/2 teaspoon vanilla extract
1/4 teaspoon baking powder
Pinch of salt

**MAKES
6**

82
calories
each

Method

Place the coconut flour in a separate bowl and add in the baking powder, coconut oil, vanilla extract and a pinch of salt and mix well. Place the eggs and bananas into a bowl and beat them until creamy. Add in the egg/banana mixture and combine until it's a smooth consistency. Stir in the apricots and mix well. Line a 6-hold muffin tin with paper cases and spoon some mixture into each one. Transfer them to the oven and bake at 200C/400F for 20 minutes. Allow them to cool. Store in an airtight container. This recipe is for a small quantity of muffins, suitable for one person but feel free to multiply the quantities if you wish to make extras.

Blackforest Milkshake

SERVES 1

297
calories
each

Ingredients

75g (3oz) frozen cherries, pitted
1 tablespoon 100% cocoa powder
Flesh of ½ avocado
100mls (3½ fl oz) milk

Method

Place all of the ingredients into a food processor or smoothie maker and process until smooth and creamy. Serve and enjoy.

You may also be interested in other titles by
Erin Rose Publishing
which are available in both paperback and ebook.

 Quick Start Guides

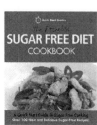

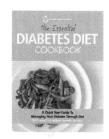

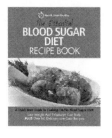

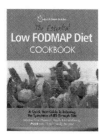

Books by Sophie Ryan
Erin Rose Publishing

30 Simple And Delicious Superfood Energy Balls And Bites
Recipes For Great Health and Wellbeing

Over 30 Easy And Delicious Superfood Energy Bars
Recipes To Boost Your Vitality

30 Simple And Tasty Energy Shots And Smoothies
To Power Up Your Health And Well-Being

Printed in Great Britain
by Amazon